Mark Scott is the Secretary of the NSW Department of Education and has a distinguished record in public service, education and the media. Initially a teacher and education policy adviser, Mark enjoyed a long career in journalism. He was editor-in-chief of Fairfax newspapers and then managing director of the ABC from 2006 to 2016.

T0363073

Writers in the *On Series*

Fleur Anderson
Gay Bilson
John Birmingham
Julian Burnside
Blanche d'Alpuget
Paul Daley
Robert Dessaix
Juliana Engberg
Sarah Ferguson
Nikki Gemmell
Stan Grant
Germaine Greer
Sarah Hanson-Young
Jonathan Holmes
Daisy Jeffrey
Susan Johnson
Malcolm Knox

Barrie Kosky
Sally McManus
David Malouf
Paula Matthewson
Katharine Murphy
Dorothy Porter
Leigh Sales
Mark Scott
Tory Shepherd
Tim Soutphommasane
David Speers
Natasha Stott Despoja
Anne Summers
Tony Wheeler
Ashleigh Wilson
Elisabeth Wynhausen

Mark Scott

On Us

hachette
AUSTRALIA

*Every attempt has been made to locate the copyright holders for
material quoted in this book. Any person or organisation that may
have been overlooked or misattributed may contact the publisher.*

Published in Australia and New Zealand in 2020
by Hachette Australia
(an imprint of Hachette Australia Pty Limited)
Level 17, 207 Kent Street, Sydney NSW 2000
www.hachette.com.au

First published in 2019 by Melbourne University Publishing

10 9 8 7 6 5 4 3 2 1

Copyright © Mark Scott 2019

This book is copyright. Apart from any fair dealing for the purposes of private study,
research, criticism or review permitted under the *Copyright Act 1968*, no part
may be stored or reproduced by any process without prior written permission.
Enquiries should be made to the publisher.

A catalogue record for this
book is available from the
National Library of Australia

ISBN: 978 0 7336 4387 3 (paperback)

Original cover concept by Nada Backovic Design
Text design by Alice Graphics
Author photograph by Quentin Jones
Typeset by Typeskill
Printed and bound in Australia by McPherson's Printing Group

The paper this book is printed on is certified against the
Forest Stewardship Council® Standards. McPherson's Printing
Group holds FSC® chain of custody certification SA-COC-005379.
FSC® promotes environmentally responsible, socially beneficial
and economically viable management of the world's forests.

*I don't think there's much point in bemoaning
the state of the world unless there's some way
you can think of to improve it. Otherwise,
don't bother writing a book; go and find a
tropical island and lie in the sun.*

Peter Singer

Peter Singer's words nagged me all summer. What if I had no solutions? What if I had run out of hope? Maybe I should have gone to the beach.

It wasn't the first time I had struggled for solutions. I ran the ABC for a decade and saw myself as being in the business of the future. We wanted to make a public broadcaster for the digital age; and for that, you needed to embrace technology and change and the opportunities of the new.

My first project on starting as managing director in 2006 was to develop a five-year plan. This will be no surprise to the ABC's critics. Such things are the hallmark of socialist collectives. But I had a five-year contract and needed to know where the organisation should head.

This step turned out to be an abject failure. I never did get the five-year plan sorted. I had come from Fairfax, a newspaper company that was getting battered by the first waves of digital disruption. I had read all I could about how digital technology would reshape media organisations and how audience expectations were changing. Almost immediately, reality swamped me. It was virtually impossible to know where the media world was going to be in five years' time. There was no clarity. It was all changing so quickly.

In 2006, you could just hope to work out the direction. It was going to be a world where content was delivered online. Faster internet speeds would allow people to watch, listen and read on their computers. New providers would emerge to deliver content, so media organisations would not need to own printing presses or broadcast transmission towers to reach an audience. There would be more choice for consumers and, as could be seen with the first wave of online news services, more choices meant smaller audiences for traditional providers.

So, rather than a five-year plan, I got a sense of direction for change. There was a line from the Italian novel *The Leopard* I liked and that I cited often as I talked with staff around the country: 'If we want things to stay as they are, things will have to change.' We needed to embrace the new opportunities on offer from technology to transform the ABC, so it would be as relevant, compelling and indispensable to future generations of Australians as it had been in the past.

I am glad we kept it pretty loose. If we'd locked in a plan, we would have missed some things in those first five years. Like the iPhone. And the iPad. The unleashing of Facebook and Twitter. And the rise of content streaming giants like Netflix and Spotify.

BuzzFeed and its listicles. And the importance of YouTube, then only a year old and set to be purchased by Google. The internet of things. And how all these businesses would work. What they would give us. And what they would ask of us.

When they first landed, we didn't understand them. They were just shiny and new and exciting. I remember in 2007 when I first saw an iPhone, which someone had purchased in the US. When we took it out of its beautiful box, it was something to behold. Sleek, expensive and beautifully designed. It reminded me of a BMW sports car: desirable, but something I was unlikely ever to get myself. When I started at the ABC, I negotiated as part of my contract that I would have a BlackBerry. That was as far as I could see technology going.

Henry Ford understood this when he revolutionised the motor car industry. 'If I asked people what they wanted, they would have said faster horses.' They asked me and I just wanted a new BlackBerry, with that nifty keyboard for my thumbs.

All that followed the iPhone unveiling was unimaginable. Genuine innovation fuelled by Moore's Law and staggering consumer demand. It didn't just change media and technology. It transformed the world. Not just because of the extent of change, but the way that these technologies and innovations were feeding each other, making the pace of change accelerate at ever-faster rates. Apple,

Google, Facebook, Amazon and Chinese counterparts Tencent and Alibaba are now on the list of the ten largest companies in the world. Others, like Twitter, dominate our political discourse. Netflix and Spotify are revolutionising what we watch and listen to, and how we do it.

I didn't anticipate any of our current reality: what it means for us to be living in this tech-transformed world. I was just very excited by all that these innovations promised to me as a consumer and also by what could be on offer to media organisations like the ABC. I had no real sense of what it all might mean to us as a community and a society. Or that our personal benefit might come at a collective cost. That was naive, but I was hardly alone. No one really understood what was being unleashed.

But now the stakes seem higher still and I am in a real business of the future, I have the curious title of Secretary, NSW Department of Education. In effect, I run one of the world's largest school systems: 2200 schools; 800,000 students; 60,000 classrooms; 130,000 on the payroll.

You need hope to do this job. You need to believe. You need to believe in the power of education to transform lives. You see it as the way to overcome disadvantage, building a fairer society. You believe you are preparing young people for a world in which they can flourish, not just survive or endure. You believe it can be a better world, with better citizens, who you have prepared in your schools.

In a sense, this was the biggest difference between running a public broadcaster and running a big education system: where you see the results. At the ABC, you could sense some of your impact on the radio today or on the TV tomorrow. But in education, so much of what is important will not be seen in this year's My School, or in next year's NAPLAN results. A society educates its children. Far from now, we will understand if we got it right.

Children starting school this year may live for another eighty years or maybe many more. I whisper in the ear of a school principal as we are about to speak to his thousand primary students in assembly: 'You are shaping 80,000 years of human life.' They will be the future of us.

A young person who starts school this year will leave our system in the early 2030s. Most likely, they will then do further learning or study. And then decades of work, most of it in the second half of the century. Good educators should be slightly obsessed about the future. What will it be like for these young people as they make their way?

At the department, we have been giving lots of thought to how best prepare young people for a changing world. What jobs will go; which new ones might emerge. What AI and automation might mean. Making our best guess at how to prepare young people for a life of ongoing learning and constant change. A world that seems to have turned more menacing, uncertain and complex.

I have sat through a lot of executive-team strategy sessions. The best advice came from a fellow named Tony Golsby-Smith, who seemed to my teams to be a bit of a mystic. Tony would always push us back to the Socratic method, emphasising dialogue and a robust dialectic. Our strategic conversations never strayed far from what the Greeks would have expected, but with butcher's paper, Post-it Notes and felt-tipped pens.

Teams always focused too much on where they wanted to be going, Tony would say. This wasn't the most important question. Before you can know where you are going and have solutions for the future, you need to know where you are today and how you got there. On these things, as we started out, there was rarely consensus.

To understand how to prepare young people for tomorrow, we need to understand where we are and how we got here. And, most importantly for me, I need to understand what I didn't see, what I didn't appreciate. What I got wrong. What we failed to see and understand. Without seeing where we came from and understanding where we are, how can you find a solution for how to prepare young people for this changing world?

In our department, we spent the second half of 2018 reviewing the policy on mobile phones in schools. Nearly all high school students have them and very many students in primary schools do as well. Did anyone see that coming, just a decade ago? Eight year olds in school with their own smartphones, able to access hundreds of millions of websites from all around the world? Phones given to them by their parents.

The arrival of the smartphone is the largest real-time experiment conducted on humanity. There is nothing to compare with this invention's expansion at such speed and with such impact on everyday life. Nearly 1.5 billion new smartphones will ship from manufacturers this year. Half the planet is connected to the internet, overwhelmingly through mobile technology using nearly 20 billion connected devices. The latest reports suggest adult users are engaging with digital media six hours a day, more than half of them doing so on mobile devices.

How do we prepare young people to live out the century in this digital world? And do we understand what has happened to us as we fell in love with our screens? What do we all need to learn?

Soon after I found my office in Sydney's ABC Ultimo tower, I found Pierre. For years, he had crafted speeches for managing directors and chairmen. He had worked at the ABC for more than a decade; this included a stint trying to produce Ian McNamara (or 'Macca') on a Sunday morning on *Australia All Over*, but I'm not sure they ever had a meeting of minds. For me, though, Pierre was a walking corporate memory. He seemed to have memorised Ken Inglis's two monumental volumes of ABC history. He found the reference, or the precedent, or the story, that helped place a moment in some historic context. He was dry, self-deprecating. One of the many colourful, quirky people who could find a home somewhere in the rabbit warren of the ABC.

Outside the office, though, Pierre was Peter Milton Walsh. His band, The Apartments, had come out of Brisbane and enjoyed great success in France, in the 1980s and 1990s. He had been an early member of The Go-Betweens, but was a little dark for Grant McLennan and Robert Forster. They observed, 'Walsh is night, we are day.'

I knew none of this as we started working together. If Pierre had a reflective melancholy, he detected none in me. When we worked together, he made the observation 'You're hard-wired for hope.' That's how I seemed, approaching this new world of opportunity. Hopeful and excited.

His observation about me was wry. Others were sharper. When I had been at the ABC for a while, a valued colleague fired a shot of simple feedback: 'You like new things.' She saw my head was quickly turned by the shiny and new—new people, new ideas, new technology. Perhaps I needed to pay a little more attention to the worth of what had been with us for a while. Have a little more respect for all that sat with us, which I seemed to overlook.

She was right. I have been taken in by new things, big promises and the hope of a wonderful future. Now I can see that in many ways over the past decade, I took all that was on offer at face value, believing in the promises and the vision, asking few questions as I dived in.

For me as a consumer, it was with newspapers that you could first see the impact of digital technology. Living in the US for a period in the 1990s, I loved their great newspapers. *The Washington Post*, *The New York Times* and *The Wall Street Journal* were all delivered to our place in the Washington suburbs. (All delivered separately, flat in a protective envelope, to the doorstep; not rolled in impossible plastic wrap, then flung in the front shrubbery, the more common experience in Australia.) These papers carried great journalism: news, features and analysis; and, come Sunday, the *Post* and the *Times* could fill half your day with their sections and magazines and supplements.

On returning to Australia, I worked at *The Sydney Morning Herald*, in the early days of dial-up internet and before news websites became a thing. I wanted to see if I could still buy a copy of the Sunday *New York Times*.

The good news was, I could. There were two newsagents in Sydney who might sell me one. But there were downsides. It would arrive ten days after publication. And it would cost me $20. I loved that paper, but not that much.

As I started working at the *Herald*, though, I understood how the system worked. The public couldn't buy *The New York Times* readily and cheaply. Fairfax bought it first, not too cheaply. The rights were several hundred thousand dollars a year. For that, the *Times* would advise the *Herald* as to the stories it was working on and then, several times a day, would send the final copy down the wires to Australia, and to other subscribers around the world. You could read a story from *The New York Times* in a Sydney or Melbourne newspaper, if the editor of your local Fairfax paper thought it was good enough, or interesting enough, to put in their local publication. He (and, in those days, the editor was always a 'he') was the gatekeeper.

In those days, gatekeepers were everywhere, not just at newspapers. The head of ABC television would decide which BBC television you could watch, working out which programs would be purchased under their BBC contract and put to air in Australia. Record labels decided which music you could buy or listen to. Of all the wonderful English-language radio content created by great broadcasters like the BBC or NPR, in the pre-digital era only a fraction was available to consumers in Australia. All the power to decide what we would watch or read, or even listen to on the radio, was with the media organisations.

The impact of the internet hit print before rolling across to broadcast media. By the time I left Fairfax to go to the ABC in 2006, most newspapers had been wrestling with a digital strategy for the best part of a decade. By 2006, the signs were obvious. Readers were abandoning print for online news. Newspapers were going to struggle to get readers to pay for online content because of the increased volume of free news available online. And, as readers went away, advertisers looked carefully at how best to spend their dollars to reach customers. There was a vicious cycle: sales falling, advertising dropping, jobs going; all leading to a less compelling proposition for purchase.

But if you were hard-wired for hope like me, how good was the new world? If you were interested in the news, it was wonderful. There was *The New York Times*. All of it, not just what a Fairfax editor allowed you to see, and now it was available to you before the print paper was delivered in New York. At first it was free; then, eventually, there was a paywall allowing a limited number of free articles before a subscription was required. But if you signed up, reading for a month every article on every device you had, cost less than I was asked to pay for one copy of that out-of-date single edition a decade before.

In fact, as the print migration to digital paced up, the critical question was how you would manage all the information that was out there for you. From all around the world. So much choice. Without the gatekeeper, who didn't know you, deciding what you would want to read. Without the space limitations of a print edition keeping good international stories out of the local papers. And much of it, nearly all of it, free.

In those early days of the smartphone, as more and more content became available online, it was hard to mount an argument that, for readers, this was not just unprece-dented and abundant. One of the things that was great about the print edition of the newspaper was that it came to you. To your home, if you had it delivered, as well as readily accessible from newsagents and newsstands everywhere. Created yesterday, read today. Of course, with the new smartphone, the news was in your hand, immediate and up to date. It made the print edition seem cold off the press.

Journalists can be sceptical about management theory, but the story of Fairfax and all declining media organisations is there in the textbooks. Big, successful organisations find it hard to renew themselves in the face of changing circumstances. The things that made you great will not keep you great. Your very success makes it hard for you to change. You cling tightly to those products or services that have delivered you profits and prosperity. You fall into denial about the reality of change that will confront you. And then, when you realise what you have lost, it is all too late.

But for those not working in newspaper companies, it was a mystery how the business worked. That most of the profits came not from what we paid to buy the paper, but from selling our attention to companies who wanted to advertise. Did most readers really understand the news was being subsidised? That someone else was always paying? That the car ads were paying for the foreign correspondents; that the job classifieds meant we could read theatre reviews? That maybe even a deep-pocketed owner, or a loathed proprietor, was underwriting what we read? Did we understand that the cost of producing what we read was much more than we had paid for it and convinced ourselves it was worth?

Every month, sales fell. Many readers migrated to read news free online or picked up the stories elsewhere if they ran into a firewall forcing payment. The challenge of getting readers to pay for stories online they had once paid for when they were in print was ferociously difficult for every media organisation in the world, although you were better positioned if you were a big global brand like *The New York Times* or *The Financial Times*.

Now the print edition is still there if you want it (although the price has steadily been jacked up—I am always shocked when I buy a copy today). And there remains some great investigative journalism. Sydney cheers Kate McClymont when she takes on the spivs and the crooks. Fearless, funny and fabulous. While if you read *The Age*, you know Nick McKenzie and Richard Baker continually come up trumps, shining light into dark places.

These have been tough times for shareholders in newspaper companies. The glory days of record profits are a memory. Fairfax has disappeared. Tough times for journos too, as thousands around the country lost their jobs. But most readers, on our phones, on our tablets, finding our own news from all around the world, seem to have moved on. I suspect it is now only old journos like me who notice when, catching a train, that everyone's head is down reading or looking at photos, but there isn't a newspaper to be seen.

Newspapers fought hard to get into the online space, but it was the arrival of social media, in particular, that meant the news could come to you even faster. You didn't have to go searching across different websites. There, in your feed, the news appeared in a steady stream, from news sources you had followed and from your friends. And again, no constraints, no gatekeepers, no limits.

Once I got into Twitter, around 2009, I would sit and watch it tick over. Stories from *The New York Times* and *The Guardian*; the ABC, *The SMH* and *The Australian*; journalists, colleagues, academics, celebrities, family members—in they dropped to my Twitter feed.

The experience of sitting there, waiting for the next delivery of tweets as I hit refresh, wondering what was to land, triggered a memory from ten years before, when I was sitting as news editor in *The Sydney Morning Herald* newsroom. At the newsdesk, monitoring the newswires as stories arrived at the paper. All the services Fairfax subscribed to: domestic services like Australian Associated Press, international services like Reuters and Agence France-Presse, stories minute by minute dropping into the system.

Fairfax was paying a fortune for these breaking news services; to know what was happening everywhere and for the rights to put these stories into the papers. But now Twitter did it for everyone, free. How good was that? Not just the feeds you had signed up for, but what your friends were posting or sending to you. At last, you were creating a personalised news service, a personalised newspaper.

When all this started to roll, when you saw your first smartphone, or video-conferenced a family member on Skype or FaceTime, or saw your joke retweeted by strangers, or began to stream or binge-watch fabulous TV series on your tablet—how could you not be an optimist about this digital world and what we had been given?

Thank you, Steve Jobs. Thank you, Mark Zuckerberg. Thank you, everyone at Google, and *The New York Times* online and all my funny tweeting friends. It was Shakespeare who said it best: 'How beauteous mankind is! O brave new world, That has such people in't!'

A couple of years back, in a fleeting nod to minimalism, the family and I decided the CD collection needed to go. It was before the big streaming services became ubiquitous, and, prior to dropping the CDs off at the Lifeline store for resale at a dollar a disc, I saved them onto a hard drive.

I remember starting the process, pulling the rarely played CDs out of their covers. And seeing the $30 price stickers. Realising I used to regularly pay $30 for a CD. Usually bought with most of the music unheard at the time of purchase. Willing to pay for the lot, drawn in by a famous name, a previous album, or a familiar track or two getting airplay. All resulting in a sizable music collection, out of which some things were played to death, and others scarcely revisited after the first listen. Suddenly, it seemed like madness.

In lots of my exploration of the new digital world, my then-teenage daughters were my test lab. I had never felt frustrated that I needed to pay for music. But they showed me how to discover music on websites like Napster. It got shut down but paved the way for the massive streaming services that followed.

Before music streaming came along, I didn't know I wanted a better deal. If Steve Jobs had asked me, I would have been happy with cheaper CDs. But these new services were remarkable. I could buy one new CD every three months; or could listen to what seemed like all the world's recorded music for three months. I could have it for nothing if

I could stomach some ads. It was all in my pocket. How could you not be sold on that?

Economists are now poring over what has happened to the music industry. If your reading tastes lead you to *The Journal of Economic Perspectives*, Professor Joel Waldfogel argued that digitisation has created a golden age of music and of other creative areas. Music has never been cheaper to produce, distribute and discover. There is more music than ever, and better quality, and happier consumers.

Revenue in the recorded-music industry has suffered a precipitous slide since the turn of the century, having fallen by more than half. And, of course, the revenue that has remained is propped up by streaming services. Revenue from physical products is a fraction of what it was two decades ago, as is digital content distribution compared to the cost of making and distributing a CD.

Waldfogel asserts that for around $10 an artist can make a song available on iTunes. Artists are no longer dependent on radio airplay or critics' reviews to find an audience. At the ABC, the triple j *Unearthed* website created a space for unsigned independent performers to upload their music. A combination of crowdsourced support and triple j curation has seen extraordinary talent uncovered, which has gone on to dominate ARIA award nominations in the following years.

I saw this happening myself with Jack, who is a son of friends of ours. He has a wonderful voice and formed a small band called Mansionair. Through *Unearthed*, YouTube, and social media support, he found a bit of an audience. And it grew from there. And grows. As I write this, I check the YouTube version of his first single. It has just ticked over 30 million plays. So, recording contracts and global opportunities for Jack, who is spending time in Brooklyn. Jack is happy. His dad can't quite believe it.

Incidentally, it is a sign you are a certain age when it is your friends' kids who are becoming famous. I remember the great *Age* editor Michael Gawenda telling me his son was in a band and was a talented muso. And it turned out, I'd enjoyed the music of the band Husky for years before I heard triple j announcer refer to Husky Gawenda, and put two and two together. I hadn't understood Michael was a *rightfully* proud father.

A lot of record companies are smaller than they were. And many of the most famous ones that were formed decades ago have now disappeared altogether. We have more music choice as consumers than ever before, and those smart algorithms listen as we listen and help us discover more music than we would have ever found on our own.

This is good news, surely, for the emerging talents like Jack, and for veterans like my old colleague Pierre. I can find all of Pierre's albums on the streaming services. But, he assures me, he will never get any real money from me and other fans listening to them. And that is not just because he was never mainstream fare. Hardly anyone gets paid meaningful dollars by these streaming services.

A blog by David Lowery (*The Trichordist*) wages a campaign against the streaming services and what they pay to artists. The payout structure is an arcane business, and the site devotes itself to improving the ethical nature of the payout. But even just some simple facts the blog proffers makes its point. Spotify pays recording labels about 0.006 cents for every song streamed. YouTube, less still: 0.0007 cents per stream. The numbers may vary. The argument doesn't.

Mansionair has done wonderfully well. But Jack isn't about to be able to support his father in retirement. A million plays of your song on Spotify might earn you a bit over $6000.

Data trackers report that 99 per cent of audio streaming is of the top 10 per cent of most-streamed tracks, meaning that all other music accounts for less than 1 per cent of the streams. More than ever, the rewards go to the biggest hits and stars. So, unless you are a huge star, you don't make much money out of selling your music; you make very little from streaming it. Your best chance to earn a sustainable living is by playing concerts. And that is incredibly hard work for many.

I went to see the American indie band Grizzly Bear play at the Sydney Opera House in early 2018. I had seen them when they last toured, as part of the Sydney Festival, and Pierre went also. One critic described their music as 'jazz-camp precision and '60s pop harmonies'. They were so tight, so accomplished, and made gorgeous sounds. 'Those boys stuck at their music lessons,' Pierre told me.

This tour, though, they were unhappy. When their latest album came out, the band's founder, Ed Droste, sounded his disquiet about the music industry today. 'This isn't to say people don't have attention spans, they do, it's just when you have everything at your fingertips for free, and there's *so much* stuff being released, it's like every week a playlist is thrown at you like "New Friday Music".' The big Spotify push is not artists' albums but playlists: steering you to music streams the algorithm thinks you will like. It's the equivalent of an automated jukebox of music programmed just for you. You may not even know who played that last track before the next one starts up.

Music just isn't viable anymore for Grizzly Bear. As I write this, I check online Droste's

progress, and see the band saying the concerts they are currently playing will be their
last for the foreseeable future. I'll miss them.
But I miss Crowded House and REM, and
many more besides. And I can always stream
their music. And Paul Kelly still records and
tours. So the news isn't all bad.

But it sobers me up. *The Journal of
Economic Perspectives* has assured me this is
a golden age. I am not paying too much for
music I am not sure I will like. My listening
is a constant discovery of the new and redis-
covery of the old. It was an industry ripe for
rationalisation, it was transformed and, as a
listener, I won. Then why don't I feel better
about it?

As I stream, I am sorry life is disappoint-
ing for Ed Droste. He deserved to be able to

play music for years. Like my friends at the *Herald* who thought they would be journalists all their lives, and should have been able to do so. It is just that I love this new world so much that I could never, ever go back to my $30 CDs or that $20 copy of the Sunday *New York Times*. Would any of us go back?

I find this a little hard to reconcile because, as I remember it, growing up in Sydney, I had little choice but it seemed to be plenty. Four morning newspapers and two in the afternoon. Radio on the AM band. Television stations: Seven, Two, Nine and Ten. Then along came SBS.

Things came and went. FM radio arrived and shook things up. The afternoon papers followed each other into memory. We lost *The*

National Times. Television programming was ever more national, with news services being local only.

But it seemed enough. I can't ever remember thinking I wanted more. You had choice, but you understood you could only read papers produced in your city. Or watch local television stations or listen to radio that was broadcast from close by. In most houses, there was only one TV and you would have to decide what to watch together.

Cable TV took forever to get to Australia. It was impeded in part by powerful commercial television owners making vast profits and sharing all that TV advertising revenue amongst themselves. When it did come, Australians remained largely immune to its charms. Despite all its investment in marketing, systems and programming, Foxtel struggled to reach more than 30 per cent of Australian homes. It was expensive, and much of what it was offering was uninspiring. The best of English-language television at that point was on free to air. The American network shows on commercial channels, the best of British on the ABC. Great foreign-language content on SBS. Foxtel, for a long time, reminded me of the Bruce Springsteen song '57 Channels (And Nothin' On)'.

But during my decade at the ABC, it all began to change. And, again, the promise of what was offered to us was extraordinary. First, more choice on free-to-air television. Digital technology meant more programs could be delivered using the broadcasting spectrum. So, multichannels emerged, first on the ABC; and then, more slowly, on the commercial networks.

The ABC grabbed the opportunity to use these additional channels to build areas of core broadcasting strength, first with the children's channel, followed closely by News 24. There was extra government funding for the children's channel, and the ABC funded the news channel by revamping the television production model, embracing new technology, changing work practices and allocating savings to build News 24.

The children's channel was largely uncontroversial, although Foxtel didn't like it because it had an entire programming suite of children's channels. But News 24 really generated heat. Sky News and its most vocal shareholder, News Corp, were loudly opposed to the creation of News 24. Australia already had a news channel, they argued: Sky News, available on Foxtel.

My argument was that if Australia were to have twenty free-to-air television channels, at least one should be a news channel, available everywhere in the country. Sky simply could not be seen in most homes, because most people were unwilling to keep paying at least $50 a month for a Foxtel subscription. With expanded free-to-air TV channels and the ABC wanting to remain the national news leader, it needed to play in the space. Through its much larger reach, News 24 brought that fevered round-the-clock news cycle to our public discourse: endless opportunities for politicians to appear, make statements, respond. All filmed, all circulated through broadcasting, and then instantly scattered on social media, triggering more response, more debate. News 24 went to air just weeks following the first Rudd–Gillard leadership spill. But, subsequently, it did cover seven federal leadership votes in the next eight years.

The battle between News 24 and Sky was an interesting microcosm of what had been a bigger debate about Foxtel and government regulation. One of the biggest reasons Foxtel had not grown was the anti-siphoning law that prohibited key sporting events being broadcast exclusively on pay TV. Much to the fury of Foxtel and News Corp executives, and despite the urgings of Rupert Murdoch, consecutive Australian prime ministers, from Keating to Turnbull, refused to give much ground on the core principle, although less popular sporting events drifted to pay TV over time.

Rupert Murdoch had turned his Sky Television franchise into a powerhouse in the UK, when it bid over the odds to get the broadcast rights to Premier League football. He built the Fox Television network in the US by smashing rights records to broadcast NFL games. He knew that exclusive sport was a TV network builder and he wanted the rules changed to boost dramatically the value of his investment in Foxtel. For decades, across different countries, Murdoch had shaped political decision-making for his corporate benefit. But in Australia, not even politicians who courted his favour could be pushed that far when it came to sport.

The argument was pretty simple. Sport was important to Australians. All Australians should be able to see it without subscribing to a service. Following the Australian cricket team's matches, or watching the AFL, the Melbourne Cup or the State of Origin— well, that was something we shared. To take part in watching sport, you just needed to have access to a TV set and be ready to watch lots of beer commercials. I suspect a few politicians would have been happy to give more ground to Rupert Murdoch on this, but the political cost was seen to be too high. These sporting events belonged to all of us.

There has been a dilution of this anti-siphoning law in recent times, reflecting the more fragmented media world. For most major sports, Foxtel offers the comprehensive package—the exhaustive coverage of nearly every event, with free to air offering select games, and the landmark events like grand finals and the State of Origin. The 2018–19 summer saw the cricket rights split. Everything would be on Foxtel. Tests and Twenty20 games would also be on Seven. For the first time in forty years, Australian one-day internationals held in this country are not on free-to-air television. The Foxtel audience for these games are much smaller than before, when everyone could watch them. The Foxtel money was too tempting for Cricket Australia to resist.

What should all of us be able to see? When I started at the ABC, I was keen we explore filming great Australian literature, and, over time, fine modern works, like *The Slap* and *The Secret River* did get adapted, to acclaim. The one I wanted most badly, though, was *Cloudstreet*, the much-loved Tim Winton novel. However, the rights to it had gone down a convoluted path and ended up with Foxtel, which developed the series. And once it had broadcast it, the ABC tried, without success, to get the rights to a screening on free-to-air TV, so that a much bigger audience could see this landmark piece of Australian storytelling. A great series that deserved to be seen by more people, but it wasn't for sale.

Having a shared space for great non-sporting Australian stories didn't attract the same political protection or interest.

Even now, it is rare for even a blockbuster program on Foxtel to attract audiences anywhere near those attracted by free-to-air television any night of the week. It is the layering of programming options that has the impact. The arrival of pay TV, even before the proliferation of streaming services, was hitting the size of free-to-air TV audiences. The evidence was in the numbers. Once ABC viewers had pay TV, it was harder to keep them watching any of the ABC channels as they once did. If they loved history, there was a channel for that. Or for science, or home renovation, or the arts. For news, there was not just Sky, but CNN, the BBC, CNBC or Fox. Each of us could disappear into our own world of viewing.

It was a harbinger. Over my decade at the ABC, all audiences for free-to-air TV were in decline, in terms of audience share and aggregate numbers. The audiences were scattering. More were catching up with viewing later, on services like ABC iview. They were watching the dozens and dozens of channels on pay TV, downloading movies and programs from Apple, and new services from Telstra and other providers. Let alone the competition from the smartphone itself, or from YouTube, or Facebook, or anything else on offer on the screen.

In so many households, everyone had a screen of their own. It took Australian television networks a long time to discover that it needed to be streaming its broadcast channels online simultaneously, so that if people had a screen in front of them, scheduled free-to-air television was an option, not just catch-up services or the internet. The TV channels needed to follow the audience to their personalised screens. No programs, news or drama or comedy rated like they used to, given the choice audiences had. Fragmentation was the buzzword. Everyone had gone their own way.

Then came the flood of streaming services, with the Australian launch of Netflix (although many Australians had found a way to watch the US version before the local launch). With Stan and the short-lived Presto, and then Amazon Prime, Australian audiences were overwhelmed with choice. Dramas, movies, documentaries, kids' series. Some of it, like the best of HBO and Showtime content on Foxtel, had big budgets, stellar casts and outstanding production values. And there was lots of other programming besides.

The arrival of streaming, in particular, addressed a major gripe Australian audiences had about local television services: the long delays in getting international programs broadcast here. The rise of piracy and illegal downloading often saw audiences for a program disappear if they were forced to wait any time at all after it was broadcast in the US or UK. The long tradition of holding back a new US program from the time of its September launch so that it was seen in Australia the following year seemed to break down. Increasingly, the world has gone same day and date—movies, music, games and TV shows released at the same time all around the world. This habit is reinforced by services like Netflix and Amazon Prime, with most of their high-profile productions, like *House of Cards* and *The Grand Tour*, available for viewing on the same day in every global market.

Netflix caters for a personalised world and it wants to understand us. Every one of us. Log in for your family and there is your icon, where you can head to your own program list. Your tastes and interests are different from your family members', so the algorithm will suggest different programs for you. And, as we watch, it is easy to forget that Netflix is a data and information company, watching us. Carefully scrutinising our viewing habits, finding patterns to create programming, and suggestions to keep us watching and paying. They know what we started to watch, when we stopped watching and which Netflix program we watched next. All providing data for commissioning, marketing and interface design. And we keep giving it more data, so it can sharpen what it offers. And perhaps one day, like pay TV, it will offer advertising, informed by all the insights offered up by 130 million paying subscribers. Alongside Disney, Netflix is the most valuable media company in the world and accounts for 15 per cent of all internet bandwidth worldwide. It released its first original drama, *House of Cards*, in 2013. Loaded with insight into its audience, it is expected in 2019 to spend $13 billion on content, most of it on original commissions.

Netflix is a global company and it soaks up global content. It does deals with broadcasters like the BBC and the ABC, investing in programs like *Bodyguard* and *Pine Gap*. It then soaks up all the international distribution rights beyond the home market. As a funding model, it seems like everyone wins. Netflix money helps with the production budget of a show. Local audiences see the show on free-to-air television and then Netflix takes it to the world. For the ABC, deals with international streaming and cable companies have been central to funding programs like *Please Like Me* and comedies by Chris Lilley.

These deals haven't just helped fund some local productions but helped Australian productions be exposed to global audiences, although they are often buried among thousands of other offerings on international streaming services. Still, this seems like more success than the ABC and other production companies long experienced in trying to sell Australian content direct to international broadcasters. Often the most popular programs made here were, by their nature, very Australian, but this made them seem quirky to international viewers. Over the past sixty years of Australian television, remarkably few local productions have translated into being big international hits.

I worried for the state of Australian drama for a long time when I was at the ABC.

Budget cuts had seen ABC drama levels fall to a record low. A revival started with some additional funding from John Howard's government, with more funding delivered later by Kevin Rudd's government. A rich era of quality followed the money—intense and demanding shows like *Redfern Now* and *The Code*; and audience favourites like *Miss Fisher's Murder Mysteries* and *The Doctor Blake Mysteries*.

What was worrying was the eroding television ecosystem supporting quality drama across all networks. To broadcast free to air, commercial television was required by law to keep local content levels at a reasonable level, but there were other ways to spend than on expensive drama programs. The higher cost of producing drama did not usually equate to boosted audience numbers bringing enhanced advertising revenue. Some of the best drama shows on commercial networks, like *Puberty Blues*, never got the audiences they deserved.

As I remember it, years ago Phillip Adams had a good joke about Australian TV. Australia hadn't had thirty years of television, he said; it had had one year of television thirty times over. Even only a decade ago, there was an extraordinary rigidity in how programs were scheduled. There was news and current affairs in the early evening, then comedy-themed nights or drama-themed nights. A mix of local and international. Variations on popular series like *CSI* and *Law & Order*.

Pressure from the digital world changed that dramatically. Commercial television is a business which seeks large audiences, hopefully to be acquired at reasonable cost. The larger the audiences, the higher the premium paid by advertisers. An hour of television is simply inventory for commercial networks to find the biggest profit they can. The cost of making local drama for commercial TV is very high, without the larger audiences to drive advertising premiums to make the cost worthwhile.

With more time-shifting following the arrival of services like iview and the commercial catch-up services, and more DVR recording allowing ads to be skipped, let alone all the YouTube and pirating outlets, there was urgent pressure to create content that had to be watched immediately. Sport was never more valuable, because it depended on being seen live. Big news events would always be a priority. But the programming that developed from this viewing habit was highly produced and, arguably, scripted: reality television.

Reality television started in waves but, after a while, it became a flood. I remember people at ABC television laughing when Channel Ten commissioned *MasterChef*, arguing it was misconceived. A dancing or music show was all about watching the talent. But cooking—that was all about tasting the food. *MasterChef* was never going to work because the audience couldn't taste the food. Simple. And very wrong. Not long after, the time of the federal election leaders debate was changed because it clashed with the season finale of *MasterChef*.

Roadblock viewing. Night after night, the reality series rolls out. The ultimate local drama, with villains and heroes and backstories and viewer favourites. Epic productions, vast, expensive enterprises—and, at times, big audiences. Real people, contrived circumstances, sometimes compelling viewing. Who will be eliminated? Watch a few episodes and it can be hard to stop (he wrote, admitting his close personal connection with the last season of *Australian Survivor*.) And if you didn't watch, you could watch others watching and get the idea of the show by viewing *Gogglebox*.

This has become the Australian content that attracts the production and marketing dollars, particularly for the commercial networks. The audiences can be very big as the season launches, if momentum builds, or if the counter programming on other networks isn't terribly tough competition. Outside sport, reality TV delivers the biggest audiences of the year.

If you don't like it, fine. There are thousands of hours of programming on Netflix for you to watch right now. (And that much more if you have decided, like me, you need to have Stan and Amazon Prime as well, to 'check them out'.)

It is so different from what we used to watch and how we used to watch it. When the ABC broadcast *SeaChange* in the late 1990s, it provided to be so popular, that when it was programmed against *60 Minutes* in its heyday, it won the ratings. Two million Australians regularly viewed every week, following life in beautiful and rustic Pearl Bay, and the professional and personal challenges besetting the beguiling Laura Gibson, played by Sigrid Thornton. It was wonderful stuff: warm, funny, engaging. 'Romantic but not a romance,' Deb Cox, one of the creators, said.

And what made it so popular? In Inglis's history of the ABC, social researcher Hugh Mackay says he thought *SeaChange*'s makers had identified a restlessness among Australians reeling from social, technological and workplace changes, and had shown the endurance of an old fantasy 'that to be a real Australian, you have to escape city life'. When you look at it that way, is it any real surprise that, nearly twenty years later, with Australians reeling ever more from social, technological and workplace changes, *SeaChange* is returning, this time on Channel Nine?

What great drama does, of course, is tell our stories. Perhaps this means we understand ourselves a little better, or understand each other a little better. One of the little programs I backed that surprised everyone with the audience it found was one that was about visiting country towns and celebrating their people: *Back Roads*, hosted by Heather Ewart. It was simply lovely stuff.

But this kind of television is increasingly rare. It is harder and harder to get the television audience numbers that would have been deemed acceptable even five or six years ago. It's not that the quality of local shows is any worse, or we are watching our screens less, but the choice on those screens is so vast and much of the global content is so good.

Who will tell the stories of us? And how important is it that we tell our stories to each other, to increase our insights, and cultivate empathy and respect for the complexity of each other's lives?

It must be expected it will be harder to get great Australian stories on air in years to come. And certainly it will be harder to reach an audience than when we first visited Pearl Bay. Commercial television networks are going to continue to argue that the local content regulations they have to abide by are too tough while Netflix has to meet no such requirements. And the Federal Government regulating local content levels on Netflix would seem heroic, given its difficulty in forcing other tech multinationals, like Google and Facebook, to pay tax.

Reduction of the local content requirements on free-to-air broadcasting seems far more likely. Australian TV broadcasters will head overseas to companies like Netflix, to find financing so that local stories can be told. And at Netflix, algorithms and data analysis drive all its decision-making. It is at its core, a technology company, using content to attract audiences, to get data to help it grow revenue. It is unreasonable to expect Netflix to do anything else. There will still be Australian stories, but they will be funded to help Netflix bolster its global library. The level of its financial investment will reflect Australia's importance to Netflix's global strategy. We're not the US, or Europe or India or China. We're third tier.

The worst possible thing would be if Australian television drama goes the way of Australian films. They are still being made, but the budgets are mainly tiny and most of us only catch one of them if it really piques our interest. The box office numbers tell the story. So many Australian films disappear without a trace, in a movie world that is increasingly dominated by the global market and blockbuster franchises, with their huge production budgets and marketing spend. And much of the very best Australian talent is working in that global market, telling global stories for global consumption. Australian governments fall over themselves competing to attract filming of blockbusters, providing employment for local actors and crews. The key to making such deals work is ensuring that in no way is it apparent that the particular film has been made in Australia.

This makes the ABC more important than ever because, unlike everyone else, the driving force behind the ABC's final decision is not simply about making money. The ABC needs to be the home of Australian conversation and culture and stories. A space for all of us, where we can come in from a world awash with choice, and find the stories of us. Told by people who know they need to reflect our nation to itself, to help us understand each other a little better.

Of course, you don't always see the consequences of things at the time you sign up to them. How Netflix might smother Australian stories. How free websites might crush investment in news. How Spotify might help musicians find audiences but make them lose income. How more for each of us could mean less for all of us. This may not be that different from how it has always been with us and the media. We used it, but we didn't really understand how it worked. The price I've paid for having all the world's media on my phone? Fewer journalists, writing for thinner papers. No more Grizzly Bear. Less local drama on TV.

I just didn't know it at the time. But I bought in fast and was easily sold on it. And if offered it again today, I would be sold on it again. I can see what I have gained, and it is only when I think hard about it that I can see what we have lost.

That is the story, isn't it? Lots of choices for each of us. But a growing sense that this might have been a bad deal for all of us. My decisions have been so simple. I like new things. Buy the device. Find the app. Sign up. Agree to the terms and conditions. (The great lie we all tell: 'I have read the terms and conditions'.) And, like all of us to some extent, I handed myself over to this tech-driven world, something embodied by that phone I never thought I would have.

The smartphone may have transformed the world, but no new service has reached so many people so quickly as Facebook. In 2006, when we were scratching away at creating a five-year plan for the ABC, there are some things we hazarded a guess at: faster broadband, streaming services, the spread of podcasts, personalisation. But no one envisaged what would happen with Facebook, then only just emerging from its chrysalis in US colleges. That it would grow so big, so fast. And, defying almost all trends and predictions, as it grew, its importance in its users' lives grew also. The numbers quickly go out of date, but the trendline has been consistent.

In October 2012, Facebook reached one billion users, and 55 per cent of them were using it daily. By June 2017, the users had doubled, to two billion, with 66 per cent of them using it daily.

I remember we at the ABC would look at the data and be astounded. Lots of journalists were on Twitter. Some, like Leigh Sales, Annabel Crabb and Mark Colvin, grew what were among Australia's largest Twitter audiences. That was where the political action seemed to be happening; the breaking news and the testy squabbles. For the political and media elite, Twitter was the forum.

But the numbers told a different story. Twitter may be the obsession of a political and media elite, but it was Facebook where the Australian public were, in vast numbers.

And it was not just about how many had signed up but how often they were on the site, every day. Facebook, with its friends, stories, pictures and videos, that constantly changing feed, became an indispensable companion to millions. Now, 60 per cent of the Australian population are active Facebook users. One in two Australians visits Facebook daily.

Those Australians aren't paying for Facebook directly, although, they love it so much, they may be willing to do so handsomely. *The Financial Times* reported research by a global group of academics that surveyed consumers to see what they would 'pay' for Facebook in monetary terms, concluding that it was, conservatively, about $42 a month. If this high daily usage is indicative of dependence, is it that surprising?

The old line was always that if you aren't paying, you're the product. As with many a media product, those paying are not the consumers but advertisers. It's just like the old days, as with commercial radio and television, where programming is free to you as long as you will endure the ads. But the power now, of course, is in the information about you, provided by you, to the advertisers, to make the advertising more targeted and effective. Half of what was spent on advertising was wasted, it was said, you just didn't know which half. Now they know much more.

And how does Facebook do this? By knowing us so well. By watching us so closely. By what we have given it. Critics have described the business as 'surveillance capitalism'. Collecting dossiers on each of us that are worthless in isolation but, with billions of new data updates daily, so valuable in aggregate when torn apart by increasingly powerful analytics tools.

As we now understand better, with all the reporting on Russian attempts to infiltrate the 2016 US presidential election, the surveillance is not just about being able to put ads in front of you for products that you will like. It is about shaping the news stories that come your way, to drive your interest and your engagement, so you stay on the site.

What you see in your feed becomes your news and your version of the truth. We know now some of it may be fake: concoctions designed to deceive. But so much of our construction of news and understanding of truth come through a layering of listening and watching and reading. If you are spending your day monitoring your Facebook news-feed and the stories are all reinforcing your world view and your version of the truth, you become more certain of its integrity and accuracy. Amidst all the news and analysis, come your friends with their updates and their pictures. You trust them and your confidence in them washes over into the other things coming to you through your feed.

And as we get more absorbed in our news feed, and more critical of other media sources and of the media in general, our critical judgment begins to wane as well. Harvard's Nieman Lab reported findings that those with negative opinions of the news media are less likely to spot a fake headline or see a distinction between news and opinion, but at the same time are more likely to believe they can find online the information they need.

Daniel Patrick Moynihan was a marvellous stalwart of the US Senate, where he served for a quarter of a century. He was a reformer and an intellect, and two of his most famous insights seem appropriate for these times. 'Everyone is entitled to his own opinion, but not to his own facts,' he said. He also wrote of the way we are always 'defining deviancy down'. We now accept things as normal that we would once never have thought of as normal. As standards and expectations slide, so do we. So much so, that we get to a point where we are having debates about whether people are entitled to their own facts.

At the ABC, we used to wrestle with these things. The editorial policies were never designed to bring false equivalence, to reduce every issue to he said/she said and different versions of the truth. Paul Chadwick, a sage thinker who was our director of editorial policies, urged our program makers to follow the weight of evidence in dealing with contentious issues. And we declared some matters closed for debate, despite some loud dissenting voices. The Holocaust was real. Vaccines were a social good. The world was not made in six days.

But on some issues, like climate change, sceptics argued loudly that advancing the mainstream scientific view was evidence of bias. All voices clamoured to be heard, irrespective of their level of insight or expertise or scientific peer validation. The organisation would be under siege with the demanding of equal time for sceptics, and when one of them made it to air, there was fury that hard questions were asked.

New books exploring this phenomenon seem to emerge monthly. Tom Nichols in *The Death of Expertise* explains how so many Americans have not only come to believe things that simply are not true but also actively resist accessing any new information that puts these beliefs under threat. In *The Death of Truth*, Michiko Kakutani speaks of how 'the wisdom of the crowd has usurped research and expertise, and we are each left clinging to the beliefs that best confirm our biases'. Her view seems validated every day. She calls out evidence of dislocation and tribalism, fear and hatred of outsiders. As we choose what media to consume or are fed what the algorithms know we will like, we create our own, not a shared, understanding of the world. It is so much harder to reach out and understand, so much harder for politicans to lead across the divide.

This is not just in the US, or Brexit-torn Britain. In Sydney, if you only listen to Alan Jones and read *The Daily Telegraph*, and keep an eye on Sky News at night, and if what you read online follows the themes pursued in your mainstream media consumption, it is likely your world view is confirmed at every turn. The same applies if you are reading the *SMH* or *The Age*, listening to the ABC and checking out *The New York Times*. I would argue these latter outlets cover a greater plurality of views, but I know this argument would be met with howls of derision from many in other tribes.

There have always been partisan media outlets. I am always interested in how the prime-time audience for Fox News seems relatively small to me: fewer than 3 million viewers—less than 1 per cent of the US population. For a long time, Fox News barked but found it hard to reach swinging voters. But now its influence only grows as its message flows out to a larger audience through social media distribution, like Facebook's newsfeed. The newsfeed overcame all the limits of television, finding independent voters, targeting people with individualised messages, stirring people who may never have voted before to go to the polls. Fox News may long have been providing the fuel, but now social media delivers the propulsion.

When Facebook first started tailoring what people could see in their newsfeed, there was some strong negative feedback. The tailoring seemed that much more insidious because, in a sense, we never really understood it was there. Your newsfeed looked like everyone else's newsfeed. But the stories you received, the messages designed to shape your thinking, were different, shaped to engage you. But, despite some noise, engagement grew. More time on the site, providing more data, delivering more targeted effective advertising, driving more revenue.

Every day that each of us is on Facebook, Facebook is learning how to keep feeding us stories to keep us on the site. Currently, the average user is there for fifty minutes a day.

The newsfeed was a device to keep us interested and coming back, so that Facebook could consume our time and attention. It triggers that satisfying spark we get when every time we look at our feed, there is something new.

At the end of 2018, a large dump of internal Facebook emails confirmed the strategy that all these decisions were based around growth. How the algorithm will push more provocative commentary and analysis your way to keep you stimulated and engaged and on the site. Facebook started as a site for college students to connect, and then, as it grew, wanted to 'connect the world'. But it basically became addicted to growth. To use Kara Swisher's phrase, it became a digital arms dealer, weaponising social media, using tools that are designed so 'the awful travels twice as fast as the good'. So that, following the attack at a Pittsburgh synagogue in October 2018, *New York Times* reporters could find thousands of anti-Semitic images and videos uploaded to Instagram, which is owned by Facebook. Nearly 12,000 had the hashtag #Jewsdid911.

In his book *World Without Mind*, Franklin Foer argues tech companies are snatching away our free will through their obsession with growth, automating our choices through our lives, shaping so many of the decisions we make. And the key to it all is what we have willingly passed over to them:

> Our data is this cartography of the inside of our psyche. They know our weaknesses, and they know the things that give us pleasure and the things that cause us anxiety and anger. They use that information in order to keep us addicted. That makes the companies the enemies of independent thought.

This is not just the view of sceptical journalists. One critic snagged my attention when he told a privacy conference that tech companies were taking personal information and weaponising it against us with military efficiency, with scraps of data—each harmless enough on its own—being assembled, synthesised, traded and sold. Profiles are run through algorithms, which serves up increasingly extreme content that pounds our harmless preferences into hardened convictions. And who was the critic? The man who sells the screens and hosts the apps that steal our time and shape our minds. Apple's CEO, Tim Cook.

Tech firms talk about engagement, but so many of us know this really means addiction. It seems a harsh word, addiction. I look up a simple definition: 'a physical or psychological need to do, take or use something, to the point where it could be harmful to you'. And as the early creators of the sites have freely admitted, they were designed using the same psychological insights that had so successfully driven addiction to things such as poker machines. It's a world we didn't know we wanted. All this new digital content fills up Infinity Pools: the apps and other sources of endlessly replenishing content. Two former Google execs, Jake Knapp and John Zeratsky, coined the term and explain it simply. 'If you can pull to refresh, it's an Infinity Pool. If it streams, it's an Infinity Pool.' A world always available; a place designed so you could get lost in it forever.

And there is something about negative emotions that means, in an online setting, they seem much more powerful in grabbing our attention, in driving a reaction, in keeping us compelled and clicking. It can be ugly, but it is hard to look away. Negative emotions spiked by algorithms inciting us, 'bad actors' seducing us, fellow citizens abusing us.

I remember that back when I was working at the *SMH*, the letters pages were always a wonderful showcase of the readers' wit and intelligence. When I started, they all seemed to arrive in the mailbag, although a few may have been faxed through to us. But there was something about having to write a letter, and address an envelope, and find a stamp and then post it, that seemed to provide breaks on the intemperate or splenetic. Once email arrived, the tone of the correspondence changed quickly and markedly. The wonderful letters were still there, but they were buried beneath a torrent of fury or abuse. It was just so easy to press 'send'; an early sign of the unleashed trolls, who would soon be abundant in the online world.

If you are not a target of such sexist, racist or abusive online attacks, it can be a surprise to learn of this stuff if it hasn't popped up in your feed. I did a panel about Twitter at the ABC, with Annabel Crabb and Mia Freedman, just as the site was beginning to generate a lot of attention. When questioned about trolls and hate speech, I was somewhat dismissive, arguing there had always been jeering, hectoring crowds and Twitter had just given them all a mouthpiece. I was astonished when Crabb and Freedman then spoke of a personal viciousness they had encountered: raw, menacing, malicious, sexual and sexist, constant. Their revelations were fearless and honest. As they spoke, I had a revelation that, about these things, I was clueless and prone to mansplaining. I later learned that some of the ABC's most respected presenters had to get off the social media sites because of targeted venom.

It has been much remarked on that Facebook worked assiduously and effectively to keep porn off its sites. Such content, while clearly finding a home on millions of websites, was not in keeping with Facebook's mass brand. The machines aren't bad in tracking it down. But diligence in detecting the fake news and the incendiary commentary seems to have come very late and haphazardly, well after people have been emboldened, encouraged and incited by content delivered on their personal feed.

How hard can it be for Facebook to control this? Pretty hard. It has tried to create posting rules. It has 7500 human moderators reviewing content posted by users, and reported either by other users or artificial intelligence: more than 10 million such questionable posts every week. They try to moderate according to Facebook's rules, with an error rate of less than 1 per cent. In a good week, the moderators might let 100,000 posts remain on that should have been taken down, and this is not even considering those that may never have been detected.

The year 2018 was one of damage control at Facebook, as the revelations of massive process failures continued. A queue of early key staff and investors criticised how far it has moved from its early aspirations, how rapacious have been its ambitions, how lax its controls, how negligent its management. How it was so determined to be important in the lives of each of us, it was indifferent to the impact of its work on all of us.

We let it do this. We gave it permission. And we continue to lay the rich personal data trail, so we can be served more compelling and relevant content that will keep us engaged. We had no understanding of the collective power of the choices each of us made.

And when we tick the box to consent to the terms and conditions, what are we agreeing to? The evidence would suggest we have no idea, not just because we haven't read them, but because we have no understanding how they are operationalised. The ABC showed as much in the analysis undertaken through its data lab by Simon Elvery. He recorded every time his phone or laptop contacted a server to exchange data. This came to 300,000 requests in a single week. In one hour on a Tuesday morning, his devices were averaging three requests a second. Not all were accessing highly personal information, but it was still valuable information to someone, all building insightful profiles of him. The media company most frequently seeking information from him? Google.

It is Facebook's great rival, but also a great counterpart in corporate surveillance. Information willingly handed over, through searches, or email content, or maps, or endless other apps that make our lives better. But that constantly give them more information on our lives, so they can serve us advertising that is more targeted or services that are more valuable to us. (*Are you sure you want to go to that shop? It's closed now but opens at ten.*)

Once the smartphone phenomenon exploded, with so many more people getting their news and information on mobiles, Facebook and Google dominated, taking up to 90 per cent of the incremental mobile advertising revenue. The money flooded in, with $27 billion in Facebook revenues in 2016. Nearly $80 billion from advertising for Google the following year. And, in being so dominant, they were crushing the old and the new providers.

So much cash siphoned up. And, incidently, so little given back. The once-dominant global industries, the car manufacturers, the consumer goods companies, were huge employers, not just huge profit makers. It was part of the social contract. But I came across a report on employment in the huge tech firms—those companies that are in the handful of the richest in the world, creating some of the richest people in the world—that said Facebook has 33,000 employees, Alphabet (Google) 94,000. By way of contrast, to run public education in NSW, just one Australian state, we have 130,000 staff on the payroll.

Facebook and Google don't just swallow up nearly all the ad revenue on mobile devices, they also circulate much of the news content that is being used to attract audience engagement. Both companies have started investing in philanthropy to promote journalism, but the sums are tiny fractions of the billions flooding in through ad revenue. In practice, the tech companies appear to be agnostic to quality. They pay no premium to the sources of original journalism. They only seem interested in engagement, whether that be through an outstanding original piece or a quick rewrite with a headline designed to attract clicks. The dollars follow the engagement, whether it be original or rewritten, months or moments in the making.

There is still great journalism, of course. There were revelations about Facebook itself—87 million Facebook profiles harvested of information to be exploited in the US presidential election and the Brexit campaign. The

#MeToo revelations all round the world. The Panama Papers. The investigations that led to the Banking Royal Commission.

But the hollowing out of newsrooms means that, invariably, there are fewer reporters to do the digging on stories that may lead nowhere, so that one day they may do the digging on a story that changes a city or a nation. There is less reporting on state government, and much less on local government. And there are far fewer specialists reporting, those who have deep contacts, read widely and vast experience, who can sense which leads to follow and know the questions to ask. But we can all comment on what is left, via Twitter.

The range of global news available may be extraordinary, and there is a hoard of blogs and newsletters and small websites, if you can find them; but the sense that there is still the deep, rich, broad, well-researched news that we once read in the paper each morning is fading fast. In my experience, while newspaper editors are in the chair, they talk up the continuing quality of their publication. Once they vacate the chair, they admit how thin the proposition has become, how ragged the staff, how fraught the times and how tyrannical the data. Now that you know what everyone reads, you need to feed them. The analytics guide your choices.

I remember watching great editors pull together newspaper editions. They would often keep a slot on page one for stories that were 'dull but worthy'. Important stories, that in a serious newspaper deserved a serious run, even if few people were going to read them. Specialist-rounds people would argue for their significant stories, and editors trusted their judgment and found a home for their yarns. Great editors looked for the story that was different, a surprising angle—effectively, a surprise for the reader. There was a belief that, often, the most rewarding stories were the ones a reader might have thought was of no interest until they read the first few lines and the journalist's storytelling craft took over.

There is limited time to invest in all that now, with the demand for the stories readers will look at in big numbers. And editors know what they are, because of all the data at hand on the online traffic that previous stories have generated. The papers today aren't as bad as old journos like me think they are, and the ones from days gone by weren't as good as we remember. But everyone who worked at them and loved them wishes there were a way they could be better today, given the financial realities of the digital world.

It feels like Neil Postman's moment.

He died in 2003, and never saw an iPhone or posted on Facebook. His most famous book, *Amusing Ourselves to Death*, was released in 1985, with the subtitle 'Public Discourse in the Age of Show Business'. In it, he argued the impact of television, and television culture, had influenced all parts of modern life: politics, education, religion, journalism.

He began with those two dystopic literary visions created in the twentieth century, Aldous Huxley's *Brave New World* and

George Orwell's *1984*. Writing just as Orwell's fabled year passed, Postman argued we had missed the real story: that Huxley was closer to the truth. Huxley and Orwell didn't prophesy the same thing: in fact, they made strikingly different observations. With Orwell, the oppression would come at us from a controlling government, from Big Brother. With Huxley, the oppression wasn't imposed. He saw that people would be oppressed by what they loved, adoring the technologies that stopped us being able to think and to understand what was happening in the world around us.

Postman explained that:

What Orwell feared were those who would ban books. What Huxley feared was that there would be no reason to ban a book, for there would be no one who wanted to read one. Orwell feared those who would deprive us of information. Huxley feared those who would give us so much that we would be reduced to passivity and egoism. Orwell feared that the truth would be concealed from us. Huxley feared the truth would be drowned in a sea of irrelevance. Orwell feared we would become a captive culture. Huxley feared we would become a trivial culture.

Postman's argument was that Huxley, not Orwell, was right. Now, we can see they were both right. We may be amusing ourselves to death, but, in doing so, the truth is being concealed; in our curated bubbles, we are being deprived of information, and are part of a captive and trivial culture.

Huxley wrote about soma, a drug people took so they would know no pain. We medicate, as he foresaw. But we also self-medicate, in our addiction to our screens. Orwell wrote of the screen, the all-powerful screen. We now live in worlds dominated by screens that we paid for ourselves. All these screens have a camera. We don't seem to be too anxious about who is watching. In a way, we seem more concerned if no one is watching or liking or retweeting.

And it is not just the great writers and thinkers of the last century who have much to teach us as we think this through. Update the prose, and it could be a critic bemoaning the world of Instagram, the Kardashians and presidential tweets, but it is Edward Gibbon writing in *The History of the Decline and Fall of the Roman Empire*:

> The name of Poet was almost forgotten; that of Orator was usurped by the sophists. A crowd of critics, of compilers, of commentators, darkened the face of learning, and the decline of genius was soon followed by the corruption of taste.

Thinking now about this past decade, it feels like a Faustian moment. Did I sell my soul to the devil for all the knowledge and pleasure available in a digital world? There was so much I didn't understand. But now I understand it a little better, and can see what I didn't understand when I was so excited and so hopeful.

Given our dismal performance predicting how all this would play out, what chance do we have of preparing all those young people to live in a digital world that will change even more quickly and dramatically? As we have constantly seen, progress is hardly predictable and linear. And these technologies: it is how they layer on each other and reinforce each other that has made them truly remarkable. Mobile technology and social distribution. Location tracking and algorithmic targeting. Another dozen years for Moore's Law to make everything ever more smaller, faster and cheaper. None of us has any idea of the world of the early 2030s, when those who start school this year will finish Year Twelve.

We have few answers for them, but we can have a better go at helping them find the right questions to ask. Maybe this is not so new. Since the time of the ancient Greeks, this is what great education has been all about. Asking the right questions. Challenging the assumptions. Seeking insights and understanding. Searching for the why. All the things so many of us failed to do over the past decade when confronted by new toys, tools and, apparently free, abundant gifts.

It doesn't necessarily require a revolution in the classroom. It is what good teachers always already do. Demand a hypothesis. Challenge the assumptions, using the data and the evidence. Press for greater insight and understanding.

The uncertainty of the future workplace means the only guarantee is insistent change and the need to learn and relearn; with the resilience that is demanded by constantly taking on the new. We need to think carefully about how the current curriculum is shaped and structured to help prepare young people for all they will face: the extent of change, the speed of change and its inevitable unpredictability.

For a long time, shorthand for how we prepare young people for the digital world was teaching them to code computers. Now we understand that the machines themselves will code. While some people will need to create and invent and code, everyone will need to engage with the technology. Given what we have seen, it would be good if all of us understood how it worked. What we can see from the Facebook experience is that there are many ethical choices behind the technology.

There have been countless examples of how biases shape the programming that impacts the outcomes we take for granted.

For decades in schools, English classes would explore how language could be deployed to manipulate meaning. Film studies showed examples of propaganda and image manipulation. Now we must help young people understand how we can be shaped by the barrage of images, text, sounds, algorithms and new experiences. We must help them to be sceptical, to be critical, to be wise. It is more important than ever.

To help them find false news and to be alert to it. To seek out facts and to know that you are not entitled to your own. To understand there is something wonderful about being different, rather than the same. To defy the algorithm and the recommendations, to live outside the bubble. To appreciate what Haruki Murakami meant when he warned against reading what everyone is reading unless you want to think what everyone else is thinking.

Critical thinking, creative thinking, computational thinking, ethical reasoning—they all become increasingly important if we are to engage with what the machines can do and the impact they can have on our lives through the choices they are programmed to deliver. The development of the autonomous car will be a technological miracle, daily driving into an ethical minefield. And someone will need to be helping decide who to keep safe: the passenger or the pedestrian; the child or the grandparent.

Maybe Huxley and Orwell will have greater resonance now than they did when I studied them at school, when they seemed to be darker minds from darker times. I suspect those lessons can come alive again. And when students read *Stasiland* by Anna Funder, I hope they stop and wonder, as I did when I heard her speak recently. Those volumes of surveillance—those Stasi files from East Germany that if laid out would have run to 180 kilometres. A country engulfed by spying. Do the citizens who survived sign up to Facebook today? If you have known the price of surveillance, do you protect your identity more, or have you given up? And, as a young person today, understanding what happened in history not so long ago, do you think a little more carefully about what you might be willing to give up and what you might want to protect?

As we seek to help young people explore new technology and its impact, we can help them ask some pretty basic questions. Some obvious ones that we didn't ask enough in recent years. Like, what is this technology designed to do? Who owns it and how do they define success? What does it say it does and what does it really do? What are the implications if the owners are successful? Who is paying? And if we are not paying, what is being asked of us? What might we gain? What could we lose? And do we need to think harder before we hand ourselves over to all that is on offer?

So much of what we need to teach children for tomorrow, I need to learn today. I suspect that is true for nearly all of us.

Over summer, I wrestled with all these things that had turned my head for a decade or so, the shiny new things. New technology, new apps, new ways of watching and listening and sharing and understanding the world. So much on offer to all of us, and how we all embraced it.

We all just made some private choices. What we wanted to read and watch and share with our friends. When everyone signed up and shared, how could we have been expected to know what the impact would be on how we tell our stories, share our news, elect our governments? I even want to excuse those who were responsible and who made their billions from us. I don't think even they understood, they just found a way to make money. But we know now.

On Netflix, Marie Kondo, the Japanese decluttering queen, popped up with a season of programs about all the problems of having too much. Houses loaded with purchases that once must have seemed a good idea. A global flood of photos appeared online as people pulled out their cupboard drawers, folded and restacked their clothes, dumped anything that didn't spark joy.

Even before the programs had gone to air, my wife had promised the family a 4-metre skip for Christmas, dropped in the driveway, so we could start an overdue purge. Inspired by Kondo, my youngest daughter dismembered our kitchen, crammed the skip and donated to the Lifeline store. Weeks later, we were still humming as we opened the cupboards and could find what we wanted. The man with the skip told me, as was reported by the newspapers, such companies were having an unusually busy new year. So many of us were throwing out what we had once wanted, needed so badly, just had to have, all of which had once seemed a good idea.

And that thirst for simplicity, for a little bit less, carries over to the technology world, of course. Having been convinced of the benefits of all of it—all the music, all the new, endless Instagram updates of photos of holidaying friends—we know it has all become too much. No one made a New Year's resolution to spend more time online. It is all about less. Less endless clicking on social media sites, having less screen time. Being more thoughtful, more deliberate, more purposeful. The new Apple iOS update gives you a tally of how much time you have spent looking at a screen. When a friend first saw her number, she knew it wasn't good—and that was when she thought it was her weekly total. When she saw it was her daily average, disquiet turned to dismay. Who of us isn't dismayed when we see such a tally? *How can I spend so much time, every day, looking at this screen?*

So much on my screens isn't sparking much joy. Like all those purchases going into the skip, I thought it was going to be more wonderful than it turned out to be. There's just too much, and a lot of what there is doesn't energise me. The family joke is that when I put on Netflix or Apple TV, I spend so much time watching previews, I often talk myself out of watching anything. Ennui descends.

I thought of these things while watching my mother-in-law when she stayed for a few days at our summer beach rental. She is partial to a bit of Netflix, but, as with many an octogenarian, isn't too fussed by any of it, and is very happy to spend an afternoon with a book, or have a night in front of the ABC. What astounded me was seeing her read the newspaper. The news that I had purchased a paper had been met with great joy. And whereas my reaction invariably was about how thin it was, this seemed to be no problem to her. It was enough. Where I flicked through it, noting the articles I had already seen online the day before, she picked it up, lay down on the lounge, and read it. Seriously read it. Starting at the front page and working systematically through. Laughing at the letters. Reading bits out loud. And then, after an hour or so, complaining how little she had got through, sternly warning me not to throw it out.

I've turned into a newspaper flipper. I tear through those pages, reading little. Some weekends, the newspapers remain unwrapped. And if I don't unwrap them, no one else in the family will. But I can't help but wonder if my mother-in-law has it right. That I don't need all those subscriptions and apps and news sources. There is enough to read in the paper, even on a slow summer's morning. There will be much there I would find interesting, if I slowed down and took the time, rather than endlessly tapping the screen, refreshing it to look for the latest. After a lifetime of reading newspapers, the latest one still sparks joy in my mother-in-law: not the news, but the experience and that it is fresh every morning.

I know that newspapers are fading away. But there is some wisdom in her deeply unfashionable attitude. The print editions will likely die with the generations that still love them. But I love the mindset that suggests for an hour, I will find interest and engagement in these pages, and, if I am not always restless for more, this will be enough.

It is interesting watching people in their eighties deal with all this stuff. Wanting to see the grandkids' pictures on Facebook. (And grandchildren remembering their grandparents could be watching them on Instagram.) Getting their heads around Netflix and remembering passwords. But, all in all, they seem less inclined to jump on the next new thing. Perhaps a little more sceptical about the gap between the promise and the delivery. And perhaps not as convinced that it is all necessary. There is a lot of news in the paper still, and only so many hours in the day. And when there are more days behind you than there are in front of you, you're a little more careful about how you spend your time.

If we aren't going to do the same, we do need to understand where we ourselves are today. We made decisions we didn't quite understand. We allowed the creation of remarkably powerful corporations that operate without social responsibility or a social conscience. We may have been negligent or naive, but others online have been craven, opportunistic and 'bad actors'. And often, when we stare at our screens, we know we are not our best selves.

I thought about this for a day or so. Should I get off? Delete and block the apps. Turn off location services. Reduce the trail. Use email that doesn't track me. Dumb down my phone and use it actually to talk to a friend.

But, like most addicts, I didn't feel ready to quit and argued with myself that I had things under control. I don't use Facebook much anymore, but that was more due to boredom than conscientious objection. My Twitter feed is active and a source of much breaking news. I like my daughters' pictures on Instagram. My location services are largely on because they make the apps better and their information sharper. I use Google Maps everywhere, if I am not using Waze (and Google owns Waze, anyway). Apple has my pictures. Spotify knows that I discovered Lady Gaga ten years after everyone else, and, unlike my daughters, does not judge me. Despite all that I now understand it costs, part of the genius of it is that it works for me.

My devices know my every move, what's on my mind, how I am today. I am willingly under surveillance. I am being catalogued. And if the analytics tools are asking the questions (and they are), I suspect they know better than I do that I am an unlikely flight risk. Just like the two billion Facebook users who would have read something about the data leak, and the exploitation of security gaps, and the channelling of fake stories, and the attempt to undermine a fair democratic process—and still logged in each day.

We are not going to give all this up. But, hopefully, we can be wiser by being slower. Give ourselves time to ask what is really important and brings us joy, and what comes hidden under the promise of the new. The best solutions will come with the right questions. We need to find what they are and ask them, and help our children to keep doing so throughout their lives. They must do better than we did, living in this world we created.